Kids Dress Up

Easy crochet pieces help kids play dress up in five popular costume sets. Furry yarn adds character to the cat and dog outfits, while glitter strands and metallic yarn enrich the ballet tutu and overskirt and royal crown. Most designs are given in two sizes, for ages 3-5 and 5-8.

LEISURE ARTS, INC. • Maumelle, Arkansas

Animals

EASY

SHOPPING LIST

Yarn

Cat, Dog, & Monkey
(Medium Weight) MEDIUM 4
[3.5 ounces, 170 yards
(100 grams, 156 meters) per skein]:
☐ Main Color - 2 skeins **each**

Cat Only
(Bulky Weight) BULKY 5
[1.5 ounces, 57 yards
(40 grams, 52 meters) per skein]:
☐ Fur - 2 skeins

Dog Only
(Bulky Weight) BULKY 5
[1.75 ounces, 55 yards
(50 grams, 50 meters) per skein]:
☐ Fur - 2 skeins

Crochet Hooks

☐ Size G (4 mm)
☐ Size I (5.5 mm)
☐ Size K (6.5 mm)
or sizes needed for gauge

Additional Supplies

☐ Yarn needle
☐ 3/8" (9 mm) wide Ribbon - 1½ yards (1.4 meters)

SIZE INFORMATION

Finished Measurements:
Headband - 2¾" (7 cm) wide x desired circumference
Paws - 6{7¼}" circumference x 6½{8}" long [15{18.5} cm x 16.5{20.5} cm]

Size Note: We have printed the instructions for the sizes in different colors to make it easier for you to find:
- Size Small (ages 3-5) in Blue
- Size Medium (ages 5-8) in Pink

Instructions in Black apply to both sizes.

GAUGE INFORMATION

With smallest size hook and Main Color, in Headband pattern,
12 sc and 9 rows = 2¾" (7 cm)
With medium size hook and Main Color, in Paw pattern,
11 dc and 5 rows = 3" (7.5 cm)
Gauge Swatch: 2¾" (7 cm) square
Work same as Headband, page 4, for 9 rows.
Do **not** finish off, continue working for Headband.

STITCH GUIDE

DOUBLE CROCHET 2 TOGETHER ***(abbreviated dc2tog)*** (uses next 2 sts)
★ YO, insert hook in **next** st, YO and pull up a loop, YO and draw through 2 loops on hook; repeat from ★ once **more**, YO and draw through all 3 loops on hook **(counts as one dc)**.

The Headband and Paws are made following the same instructions for all three animals.

HEADBAND

With smallest size hook and Main Color, ch 13.

Row 1: Sc in second ch from hook and in each ch across: 12 sc.

Row 2: Ch 1, turn; sc in BLO of first sc ***(Fig. 2, page 30)***, sc in FLO of next sc, ★ sc in BLO of next sc, sc in FLO of next sc; repeat from ★ across.

Repeat Row 2 for pattern until Headband measures approximately 18{19}"/45.5{48.5} cm from beginning ch **or** to desired circumference.

Finish off leaving a long end for sewing.

Fold Headband in half. Whipstitch ends together ***(Fig. 8a, page 31)***.

See individual animal for Ears.

PAW (Make 2)

With medium size hook, Main Color, and leaving a long end for sewing, ch 26{32}.

Row 1 (Right side)**:** Dc in fourth ch from hook **(3 skipped chs count as first dc)** and in each ch across: 24{30} dc.

Note: Loop a short piece of yarn around any stitch to mark Row 1 as **right** side.

Rows 2 thru 10{12}: Ch 3 **(counts as first dc, now and throughout)**, turn; dc in FLO of next dc ***(Fig. 2, page 30)***, ★ dc in BLO of next dc, dc in FLO of next dc; repeat from ★ across.

Finish off leaving a long end for sewing.

CAT & DOG ONLY - FUR

Row 1: With **right** side of Paw facing throughout and medium size hook, join Fur with slip st around second dc on Row 2; ★ ch 3, skip next dc, slip st around next dc; repeat from ★ across.

Row 2: Ch 3, turn; slip st around first dc on next row, ★ ch 3, skip next dc, slip st around next dc; repeat from ★ across to last dc, leave last dc unworked.

Row 3: Ch 3, turn; slip st around second dc on next row; ★ ch 3, skip next dc, slip st around next dc; repeat from ★ across.

Size Small Only: Finish off.

Size Medium Only - Row 4: Repeat Row 2; finish off.

ASSEMBLY (All Animals)

Fold Paw in half with **wrong** side together. With one long end, whipstitch across first 6{7} dc ***(Fig. 8a, page 31)***; secure end.
Using the second long end, whipstitch across leaving 5 rows unsewn for the thumb opening; secure end.

For second Paw, whipstitch seam in same manner making a right and left Paw.

CAT

EAR (Make 2)

With largest size hook, holding one strand **each** of Main Color and Fur together, and leaving a long end for sewing, ch 10.

Row 1 (Right side)**:** Dc in fourth ch from hook **(3 skipped chs count as first dc)** and in each ch across: 8 sts.

Note: Loop a short piece of yarn around any stitch to mark Row 1 as **right** side.

Row 2: Ch 2 **(does not count as a st)**, turn; skip first dc, dc in next 6 dc, leave last dc unworked.

Row 3: Ch 2, turn; skip first dc, dc in next 5 dc.

Row 4: Ch 2, turn; skip first dc, ★ YO, insert hook in **next** dc, YO and pull up a loop, YO and draw through 2 loops on hook; repeat from ★ 3 times **more**, YO and draw through all 5 loops on hook; finish off.

Using photo as a guide for placement, sew Ears to Headband.

TAIL

Rnd 1 (Right side)**:** With largest size hook and holding one strand **each** of Main Color and Fur together, ch 2, (sc, hdc, 4 dc) in second ch from hook; do **not** join: 6 sts.

Working in continuous rnds, dc in each dc around until Tail measures approximately 16" (40.5 cm).

Loops: Ch 3, flatten last rnd, slip st in first dc on back layer, ★ ch 3, slip st in next dc on front layer, ch 3, slip st in next dc on back layer; repeat from ★ once **more**; finish off.

TUMMY

With largest size hook, holding one strand **each** of Main Color and Fur together, ch 8.

Rnd 1 (Right side)**:** 2 Dc in fourth ch from hook **(3 skipped chs count as first dc)**, dc in next 3 chs, 3 dc in last ch; working in free loops of beginning ch ***(Fig. 3, page 30)***, dc in next 3 chs; join with slip st to first dc: 12 dc.

Note: Loop a short piece of yarn around any stitch to mark Rnd 1 as **right** side.

Rnd 2: Ch 3 **(counts as first dc)**, dc in same st as joining, 2 dc in next dc and in each dc around; join with slip st to first dc: 24 dc.

Rnd 3: Ch 3, dc in same st as joining and in next dc, (2 dc in next dc, dc in next dc) around; join with slip st to first dc: 36 dc.

Rnd 4: Ch 3, dc in same st as joining and in next 2 dc, (2 dc in next dc, dc in next 2 dc) around; join with slip st to first dc, finish off: 48 dc.

To join Tail and Tummy, weave ribbon through loops on last row of Tail and through dc on **wrong** side of Tummy; tie ribbon in a bow at side.

DOG

EAR (Make 2)

With largest size hook, holding one strand **each** of Main Color and Fur together, and leaving a long end for sewing, ch 10.

Row 1 (Right side)**:** Dc in fourth ch from hook **(3 skipped chs count as first dc)** and in each ch across: 8 dc.

Note: Loop a short piece of yarn around any stitch to mark Row 1 as **right** side.

Rows 2 and 3: Ch 3 **(counts as first dc)**, turn; dc in next 7 dc.

Row 4: Ch 2 **(does not count as a st)**, turn; skip first dc, dc in next 6 dc, leave last dc unworked.

Row 5: Ch 2, turn; skip first dc, dc in next 5 dc; finish off.

Using photo as a guide for placement and matching beginning ch to top edge of Headband, sew Ears in place.

TAIL

Rnd 1 (Right side)**:** With largest size hook and holding one strand **each** of Main Color and Fur together, ch 4, 3 dc in fourth ch from hook; join with slip st to top of beginning ch: 4 sts.

Rnd 2: Ch 1, (sc, hdc) in same st as joining, 2 dc in each of next 3 dc; do **not** join: 8 sts.

Working in continuous rnds, dc in each st around until Tail measures approximately 8" (20.5 cm).

Loops: Ch 3, flatten last rnd, slip st in first dc on back layer, ★ ch 3, slip st in next dc on front layer, ch 3, slip st in next dc on back layer; repeat from ★ 2 times **more**; finish off.

TUMMY

Work same as Cat, page 5.

To join Tail and Tummy, weave ribbon through loops on last row of Tail and through dc on **wrong** side of Tummy; tie ribbon in a bow at side.

MONKEY

EAR (Make 2)

With medium size hook, Main Color, and leaving a long end for sewing, ch 15.

Row 1 (Right side)**:** Dc in fourth ch from hook **(3 skipped chs count as first dc)** and in each ch across: 13 dc.

Note: Loop a short piece of yarn around any stitch to mark Row 1 as **right** side.

Rows 2 and 3: Ch 3 **(counts as first dc)**, turn; dc in next dc and in each dc across.

Row 4: Ch 2 **(does not count as a st)**, turn; skip first dc, dc2tog, dc in next 7 dc, dc2tog, leave last dc unworked: 9 dc.

Row 5: Ch 2, turn; skip first dc, dc2tog, dc in next 3 dc, dc2tog, ch 2, slip st in last dc; finish off.

Using photo as a guide for placement and gathering bottom edge of Ears, sew Ears to Headband.

TAIL

Rnd 1 (Right side)**:** With medium size hook and Main Color, ch 2, (sc, hdc, 4 dc) in second ch from hook; do **not** join: 6 sts.

Working in continuous rnds, dc in each st around until Tail measures approximately 16" (40.5 cm).

Loops: Ch 3, flatten last rnd, slip st in first dc on back layer, ★ ch 3, slip st in next dc on front layer, ch 3, slip st in next dc on back layer; repeat from ★ once **more**; finish off.

TUMMY

With medium size hook and Main Color, ch 10.

Rnd 1 (Right side)**:** 2 Dc in fourth ch from hook **(3 skipped chs count as first dc)**, dc in next 5 chs, 5 dc in last ch; working in free loops of beginning ch ***(Fig. 3, page 30)***, dc in next 5 chs, 2 dc in next ch; join with slip st to first dc: 20 dc.

Note: Loop a short piece of yarn around any stitch to mark Rnd 1 as **right** side.

Rnd 2: Ch 3 **(counts as first dc, now and throughout)**, dc in same st as joining, 2 dc in each of next 3 dc, dc in next 3 dc, 2 dc in each of next 7 dc, dc in next 3 dc, 2 dc in each of last 3 dc; join with slip st to first dc: 34 dc.

Rnd 3: Ch 3, 2 dc in next dc, (dc in next dc, 2 dc in next dc) 3 times, dc in next 4 dc, 2 dc in next dc, (dc in next dc, 2 dc in next dc) 6 times, dc in next 4 dc, 2 dc in next dc, (dc in next dc, 2 dc in next dc) twice; join with slip st to first dc: 48 dc.

Rnd 4: Ch 3, dc in same st as joining, ★ † (dc in FLO of next dc, dc in BLO of next dc) twice, dc in FLO of dc just worked into †, (dc in BLO of next dc, dc in FLO of next dc) twice, dc in BLO of dc just worked into; repeat from ★ 4 times **more**, then repeat from † to † once, dc in BLO of next dc, dc in FLO of next dc, dc in BLO of next dc; join with slip st to first dc, finish off: 60 dc.

To join Tail and Tummy, weave ribbon through spaces on last row of Tail and through **wrong** side of dc on Tummy; tie ribbon in a bow at side.

Ballerina Set

EASY

SHOPPING LIST

Yarn (Medium Weight) 4

Tutu & Flowers

[5.3 ounces, 518 yards (150 grams, 473 meters) per skein]:

☐ 2{3} skeins

Note: The photo model is made using a self-striping brushed acrylic yarn that has a cotton slub that makes it airy. It also has a metallic strand that runs through it.

Headband & Leg Warmers

[2.8 ounces, 160 yards (80 grams, 146 meters) per skein]:

☐ 2 skeins

Note: The photo model is made using a yarn that has a metallic strand that runs through it to make it sparkle.

Crochet Hooks

☐ Size H (5 mm)

☐ Size J (6 mm)
or sizes needed for gauge

Additional Supplies

☐ Yarn needle

☐ ¼" (6 mm) wide Ribbon - 1½ yards (1.4 meters)

SIZE INFORMATION

Finished Measurements:

Tutu - 8½{10}"/21.5{25.5} cm long with an adjustable waist

Headband - ¾" wide x 8{9¾}" long [1.9 cm x 20.5{25} cm excluding ties

Leg Warmers - 8¼{9½}"/21{24} cm circumference

Size Note: We have printed the instructions for the sizes in different colors to make it easier for you to find:

- Size Small (ages 3-5) in Blue
- Size Medium (ages 5-8) in Pink

Instructions in Black apply to both sizes.

GAUGE INFORMATION

TUTU

With larger size hook, 5 Shells = 7" (17.75 cm)

Gauge Swatch: 7½" (19 cm) wide

With larger size hook, ch 25.

Row 1: (2 Dc, ch 1, 2 dc) in sixth ch from hook **(5 skipped chs count as first dc plus 2 skipped chs)**, ★ skip next 3 chs, (2 dc, ch 1, 2 dc) in next ch **(Shell made)**; repeat from ★ across to last 3 chs, skip next 2 chs, dc in last ch: 5 Shells and 2 dc.

Rows 2-4: Ch 3 **(counts as first dc)**, turn; skip next 2 dc, (2 dc, ch 1, 2 dc) in next ch-1 sp, ★ skip next 4 dc, (2 dc, ch 1, 2 dc) in next ch-1 sp; repeat from ★ across to last 3 dc, skip next 2 dc, dc in last dc.

Finish off.

HEADBAND & LEG WARMERS

In pattern, with larger size hook, 14 sts = 4" (10 cm)

Gauge Swatch: 4" (10 cm) wide

With larger size hook, ch 15.

Row 1: Sc in second ch from hook, dc in next ch, (sc in next ch, dc in next ch) across: 14 sts.

Rows 2-4: Ch 1, turn; sc in first dc, dc in next sc, (sc in next dc, dc in next sc) across.

Finish off.

STITCH GUIDE

FRONT POST DOUBLE CROCHET
(abbreviated FPdc)
YO, insert hook from **front** to **back** around post of st indicated ***(Figs. 4a & b, page 30)***, YO and pull up a loop (3 loops on hook), (YO and draw through 2 loops on hook) twice.

BACK POST DOUBLE CROCHET
(abbreviated BPdc)
YO, insert hook from **back** to **front** around post of st indicated ***(Figs. 5a & b, page 31)***, YO and pull up a loop (3 loops on hook), (YO and draw through 2 loops on hook) twice.

TUTU

With larger size hook, ch 100; being careful **not** to twist ch, join with slip st to form a ring.

Rnd 1: Ch 3 **(counts as first dc, now and throughout)**, dc in next ch and in each ch around; join with slip st to first dc: 100 dc.

Rnd 2: Ch 3, (dc, ch 1, dc) in next dc and in each dc around, dc in same dc as first dc, sc in first dc to form last ch-1 sp: 100 ch-1 sps.

Rnd 3: Ch 3, dc in last ch-1 sp made, skip next 2 dc, ★ (2 dc, ch 1, 2 dc) in next ch-1 sp, skip next 2 dc; repeat from ★ around, 2 dc in same sp as first dc, sc in first dc to form last ch-1 sp.

Rnd 4: Ch 3, dc in last ch-1 sp made, skip next 4 dc, ★ (2 dc, ch 1, 2 dc) in next ch-1 sp **(Shell made)**, skip next 4 dc; repeat from ★ around, 2 dc in same sp as first dc, sc in first dc to form last ch-1 sp: 100 Shells.

Repeat Rnd 4 until piece measures approximately 8½{10}"/21.5{25.5} cm from beginning ch.

Finish off.

Weave ribbon through dc on Rnd 1 and tie in a bow.

HEADBAND

With larger size hook, make a chain 28{31}"/71{78.5} cm long.

Row 1: Working in back ridge of beginning ch ***(Fig. 1, page 30)***, sc in second ch from hook, dc in next ch, (sc in next ch, dc in next ch) 13{16} times, leave remaining chs unworked for first tie: 28{34} sts.

Row 2: Ch 1, turn; sc in first dc, dc in next sc, (sc in next dc, dc in next sc) across; make a chain the same length as the first tie; finish off.

FLOWER (Make 2)

Foundation Rnd: With smaller size hook and leaving a long end for sewing, ch 3, (dc, ch 2, slip st) in third ch from hook: 2 sps.

Rnd 1 (Right side)**:** Slip st in first sp, ch 4, (dc, ch 1) 15 times in same sp, (dc, ch 1) 16 times in last sp; join with slip st to third ch of beginning ch-4; finish off.

Insert one tie up through first sp on Foundation Rnd of one Flower, over first dc, then back down to form center of Flower. Insert tie through Headband between rows.

Using long end on Flower, tack it in place to Headband.

Repeat on opposite side of Headband.

LEG WARMER (Make 2)

BOTTOM RIBBING

With smaller size hook, ch 26{30}; being careful **not** to twist ch, join with slip st to form a ring.

Rnd 1 (Right side)**:** Ch 3 **(counts as first dc, now and throughout)**, dc in next ch and in each ch around; join with slip st to first dc: 26{30} dc.

Rnd 2: Ch 2, work FPdc around next dc, (work BPdc around next dc, work FPdc around next dc) around; join with slip st to top of beginning ch-2; do **not** finish off.

BODY

Change to larger size hook.

Rnd 1: Sc in same st as joining and in next 1{2} st(s), **[**2 sc in next st, sc in next 7{8} sts**]** 3 times; do **not** join: 29{33} sc.

Working in continuous rnds, (sc in next st, dc in next st) around until Leg Warmer measures approximately 8{10}"/20.5{25.5} cm from beginning ch **or** to desired length; do **not** finish off.

TOP RIBBING

Change to smaller size hook.

Rnd 1: Slip st in next st, ch 3, dc in next 1{2} st(s), **[**skip next st, dc in next 8{9} sts**]** 3 times; join with slip st to first dc: 26{30} dc.

Rnd 2: Ch 2, work FPdc around next dc, (work BPdc around next dc, work FPdc around next dc) around; join with slip st to top of beginning ch-2, finish off.

FLOWER (Make 2)

Work same as Headband, page 10.

Sew a Flower to top of each Leg Warmer using same color as Leg Warmer and working around center dc on Foundation rnd of Flower.

Princess Set

EASY

Crown

SHOPPING LIST

Yarn (Medium Weight) MEDIUM 4

Note: A yarn with sheen makes this crown extra special.

[2.5 ounces, 197 yards (70 grams, 180 meters) per skein]:

☐ Main Color (Variegated) - 1 skein

[3 ounces, 252 yards (85 grams, 230 meters) per skein]:

☐ Contrasting Color (Blue) - 1 skein

Crochet Hook

☐ Size G (4 mm)
or size needed for gauge

Additional Supplies

☐ Safety pin

SIZE INFORMATION

Size	Finished Circumference
Small	17½" (44.5 cm)
Medium	19" (48.5 cm)

Size Note: We have printed the instructions for the sizes in different colors to make it easier for you to find:

- Size Small (ages 3-5) in Blue
- Size Medium (ages 5-8) in Pink

Instructions in Black apply to both sizes.

GAUGE INFORMATION

19 dc = 4" (10 cm)

Gauge Swatch: 4" (10 cm) wide

Ch 21.

Row 1: Dc in fourth ch from hook **(3 skipped chs count as first dc)** and in each ch across: 19 dc.

Rows 2-4: Ch 3 **(counts as first dc)**, turn; dc in next dc and in each dc across. Finish off.

STITCH GUIDE

TREBLE CROCHET ***(abbreviated tr)***
YO twice, insert hook in sp indicated, YO and pull up a loop (4 loops on hook), (YO and draw through 2 loops on hook) 3 times; push tr toward the front.

POPCORN (uses one dc)
Work 5 dc in dc indicated, drop loop from hook, insert hook in first dc of 5-dc group, hook dropped loop and draw through st ***(Fig. A)***.

Fig. A

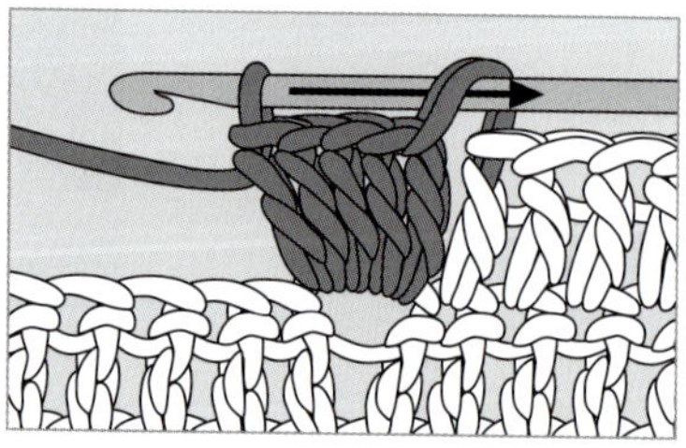

FRONT POST DOUBLE CROCHET ***(abbreviated FPdc)***
YO, insert hook from **front** to **back** around post of dc indicated ***(Figs. 4a & b, page 30)***, YO and pull up a loop (3 loops on hook), (YO and draw through 2 loops on hook) twice.

BACK POST DOUBLE CROCHET ***(abbreviated BPdc)***
YO, insert hook from **back** to **front** around post of st indicated ***(Figs. 5a & b, page 31)***, YO and pull up a loop (3 loops on hook), (YO and draw through 2 loops on hook) twice.

PICOT
Ch 3, slip st in third ch from hook.

CROWN

With Main Color, ch 84{90}; being careful **not** to twist ch, join with slip st to form a ring.

Rnd 1 (Right side)**:** Ch 1, sc in each ch around; join with slip st to first sc: 84{90} sc.

Note: *Loop a short piece of yarn around any stitch to mark Rnd 1 as* ***right*** *side.*

Rnd 2: Ch 3 **(counts as first dc, now and throughout)**, dc in next sc and in each sc around; join with slip st to first dc, drop yarn to **right** side. Slip loop from hook onto safety pin to keep piece from unraveling while working the next rnd.

Rnd 3: With **right** side facing, skip first 4 dc and join Contrasting Color with dc in next dc ***(see Joining With Dc, page 30)***; 4 dc in same st, drop loop from hook, insert hook in first dc of 5-dc group, hook dropped loop and draw through st ***(Fig. A)*** **(first Popcorn made)**, ch 5, skip next 5 dc, (work Popcorn in next dc, ch 5, skip next 5 dc) around; join with slip st to first Popcorn, finish off: 14{15} Popcorns and 14{15} ch-5 sps.

Rnd 4: With **right** side facing and working in **front** of chs on previous rnd ***(Fig. 6, page 31)***, slip loop from safety pin onto hook; ch 3, dc in next 3 dc on Rnd 2, sc in next Popcorn on Rnd 3, (dc in next 5 dc on Rnd 2, sc in next Popcorn on Rnd 3) around to last dc on Rnd 2, dc in last dc; join with slip st to first dc: 84{90} sts.

Rnd 5: Ch 3, dc in next dc and in each st around; join with slip st to first dc.

Rnd 6: Ch 1, sc in same st as joining and in next 3 dc, † slip st in next dc, ch 1, skip next dc, (dc, ch 1) 4 times in next dc, skip next dc, slip st in next dc †, sc in next 5 dc, slip st in next dc, ch 1, skip next dc, (dc, ch 1) 3 times in each of next 2 dc, skip next dc, slip st in next dc, sc in next 5 dc, repeat from † to † once, sc in next 4 dc, slip st in each dc across; join with slip st to first sc, slip loop from hook onto safety pin: 18 sc and 14 ch-1 sps.

Begin working in rows.

Row 1: With **right** side facing, skip first sc and join Contrasting Color with sc in next sc ***(see Joining With Sc, page 30)***, † ch 2, skip next 3 sts, sc in next ch-1 sp, ch 2, [(tr, slip st) in next ch-1 sp, ch 2] 3 times, sc in next ch-1 sp, ch 2, skip next 3 sts, sc in next sc †, ch 2, skip next 3 sts, sc in next ch-1 sp, ch 2, [(tr, slip st) in next ch-1 sp, ch 2] 5 times, sc in next ch-1 sp, ch 2, skip next 3 sts, sc in next sc, repeat from † to † once, leave remaining sts unworked, finish off.

Row 2: With **right** side facing, slip loop from safety pin onto hook, ch 1, sc in same st as joining, sc in next sc on Row 1, working in **front** of chs on previous rnd, † sc in next skipped sc on Rnd 6, sc in next sc on Row 1, work FPdc around next dc on Rnd 6, (sc in next tr on Row 1, work FPdc around next dc on Rnd 6) 3 times, sc in next sc on Row 1, sc in second skipped sc on Rnd 6, sc in next sc on Row 1 †, sc in next skipped sc on Rnd 6, sc in next sc on Row 1, work FPdc around next dc on Rnd 6, (sc in next tr on Row 1, work FPdc around next dc on Rnd 6) 5 times, sc in next sc on Row 1, sc in second skipped sc on Rnd 6, sc in next sc on Row 1, repeat from † to † once, sc in next sc on Rnd 6, leave remaining slip sts on Rnd 6 unworked.

Row 3: Work Picot, **turn**; skip first 4 sc, (work BPdc around next post st, work Picot, skip next sc) 4 times, slip st in next 2 sc, work Picot, skip next 2 sc, work BPdc around next post st, work Picot, (skip next sc, work BPdc around next post st, ch 4, slip st in fourth ch from hook) 3 times, (skip next sc, work BPdc around next post st, work Picot) twice, skip next 2 sc, slip st in next 2 sc, work Picot, (skip next sc, work BPdc around next post st, work Picot) 4 times, skip next 3 sts, slip st in last sc; finish off.

Cape

SHOPPING LIST

Yarn (Medium Weight)

[4 ounces, 204 yards (113 grams, 187 meters) per skein]:

☐ Main Color - 4 skeins

☐ Contrasting Color - 80 yards (73 meters)

Crochet Hook

☐ Size J (6 mm) **or** size needed for gauge

SIZE INFORMATION

Size	Finished Measurements
Small	37" wide x 20" long (94 cm x 51 cm)
Medium	40" wide x 23" long (101.5 cm x 58.5 cm)

Size Note: We have printed the instructions for the sizes in different colors to make it easier for you to find:

- Size Small (ages 3-5) in Blue
- Size Medium (ages 5-8) in Pink

Instructions in Black apply to both sizes.

GAUGE INFORMATION

In pattern, with Main Color,
4 repeats = 3" (7.5 cm),
10 rows = 3½" (9 cm)

Gauge Swatch: 3½" (9 cm) square
With Main Color, ch 15.
Work same as Body for 10 rows: 4 ch-2 sps.
Finish off.

BODY

With Main Color, ch 147{159}.

Row 1: Hdc in second ch from hook, (sc, ch 2, dc) in next ch, ★ skip next 2 chs, (sc, ch 2, dc) in next ch; repeat from ★ across to last 3 chs, skip next 2 chs, hdc in last ch: 48{52} ch-2 sps.

Row 2: Ch 1, turn; hdc in first hdc, (sc, ch 2, dc) in each ch-2 sp across to last 2 sts, skip next sc, hdc in last hdc.

Repeat Row 2 until Body measures approximately 19½{22½}"/49.5{57} cm from beginning ch.

Finish off.

Edging Rnd (Right side)**:** Turn; join Contrasting Color with sc in last hdc made ***(see Joining With Sc, page 30)***, ch 2, dc in same st, (sc, ch 2, dc) in each of next 9 ch-2 sps, (dc in next ch-2 sp, ch 1) across to last 9 ch-2 sps to form eyelets, (sc, ch 2, dc) in each of last 9 ch-2 sps; skip next sc, (sc, ch 2, dc) in last hdc and evenly across end of rows and in ch-2 sps across bottom edge, (sc, ch 2, dc) evenly across end of rows on remaining edge; join with slip st to first sc, finish off.

Tack first and last dc of eyelets on top edge of Edging together.

TIE

With Contrasting Color, chain a 44{47}"/112{119.5} cm length; slip st in back ridge of second ch from hook and each ch across ***(Fig. 1, page 30)***; finish off.

Weave Tie through ch-1 sps (eyelets) on Edging Rnd.

Sweetheart Overskirt

SHOPPING LIST

Yarn

(Fine Weight) FINE 2
[1.75 ounces, 202 yards
(50 grams, 185 meters) per skein]:
☐ Main Color - 3{4} skeins

(Medium Weight) MEDIUM 4
☐ Contrasting Color (for Tie) - 16 yards (14.5 meters)

Crochet Hooks

☐ Size E (3.5 mm)

☐ Size H (5 mm)
or sizes needed for gauge

SIZE INFORMATION

Size	Finished Measurements
Small	25" waist x 10" long (63.5 cm x 25.5 cm)
Medium	30" waist x 14" long (76 cm x 35.5 cm)

Note: Waistband will be gathered to a smaller measurement.

Size Note: We have printed the instructions for the sizes in different colors to make it easier for you to find:
- Size Small (ages 3-5) in Blue
- Size Medium (ages 5-8) in Pink

Instructions in Black apply to both sizes.

GAUGE INFORMATION

With smaller size hook and Main Color, 12 sc = 2½" (6.25 cm)

In pattern, with larger size hook and Main Color, one repeat = 3½" (9 cm)

Gauge Swatch #1: 5¼" (13.25 cm) wide

With smaller size hook and Main Color, ch 26.

Work same as Waistband: 25 sc.

Finish off.

Gauge Swatch #2: 7" (17.75 cm) wide

With larger size hook and Main Color, ch 38.

Row 1: Sc in second ch from hook and in each ch across: 37 sc.

Row 2: Ch 1, turn; sc in first sc, ch 1, skip next sc, sc in next sc, ch 3, skip next 3 sc, sc in next sc, ch 5, skip next 5 sc, sc in next sc, (ch 3, skip next 3 sc, sc in next sc) 3 times, ch 5, skip next 5 sc, sc in next sc, ch 3, skip next 3 sc, sc in next sc, ch 1, skip next sc, sc in last sc.

Rows 3-8: Work same as Body Rows 3-8.

Finish off.

STITCH GUIDE

CLUSTER (uses 4 dc)

★ YO, insert hook in **next** dc, YO and pull up a loop, YO and draw through 2 loops on hook; repeat from ★ 3 times **more**, YO and draw through all 5 loops on hook.

PICOT

Ch 3, slip st in third ch from hook.

WAISTBAND

With smaller size hook and Main Color, ch 122{146}.

Row 1: Sc in second ch from hook and in each ch across: 121{145} sc.

Row 2 (Eyelet rnd)**:** Ch 4 **(counts as first dc plus ch 1)**, turn; skip next sc, dc in next sc, (ch 1, skip next sc, dc in next sc) across: 61{73} dc and 60{72} ch-1 sps.

Row 3: Ch 1, turn; sc in each dc and in each ch-1 sp across; do **not** finish off: 121{145} sc.

BODY

Row 1: Using larger size hook, ch 1, turn; sc in first sc, (ch 3, skip next 2 sc, sc in next sc) across: 40{48} ch-3 sps.

Row 2: Ch 1, turn; sc in first sc, ch 1, sc in next ch-3 sp, ch 3, sc in next ch-3 sp, ch 5, sc in next ch-3 sp, ★ (ch 3, sc in next ch-3 sp) 3 times, ch 5, sc in next ch-3 sp; repeat from ★ across to last ch-3 sp, ch 3, sc in last ch-3 sp, ch 1, sc in last sc: 41{49} sps.

Row 3: Ch 3 **(counts as first dc, now and throughout)**, turn; dc in first sc, ch 5, skip next ch-1 sp, sc in next ch-3 sp, (4 dc, ch 1, 4 dc) in next ch-5 sp, sc in next ch-3 sp, ★ (ch 3, sc in next ch-3 sp) twice, (4 dc, ch 1, 4 dc) in next ch-5 sp, sc in next ch-3 sp; repeat from ★ across to last ch-1 sp, ch 5, skip last ch-1 sp, 2 dc in last sc.

Row 4: Ch 1, turn; sc in first dc, ch 1, sc in next ch-5 sp, ch 3, skip next sc, work Cluster, 4 dc in next ch-1 sp, work Cluster, ch 3, ★ sc in next ch-3 sp, ch 5, sc in next ch-3 sp, ch 3, skip next sc, work Cluster, 4 dc in next ch-1 sp, work Cluster, ch 3; repeat from ★ across to last ch-5 sp, sc in last ch-5 sp, ch 1, skip next dc, sc in last dc.

Row 5: Ch 3, turn; 4 dc in next ch-1 sp, sc in next ch-3 sp, ch 5, skip next Cluster, work Cluster, ch 5, sc in next ch-3 sp, ★ (4 dc, ch 1, 4 dc) in next ch-5 sp, sc in next ch-3 sp, ch 5, skip next Cluster, work Cluster, ch 5, sc in next ch-3 sp; repeat from ★ across to last ch-1 sp, 4 dc in last ch-1 sp, dc in last sc.

Row 6: Ch 3, turn; dc in first dc, work Cluster, ch 3, sc in next ch-5 sp, ch 5, sc in next ch-5 sp, ch 3, skip next sc, work Cluster, ★ 4 dc in next ch-1 sp, work Cluster, ch 3, sc in next ch-5 sp, ch 5, sc in next ch-5 sp, ch 3, skip next sc, work Cluster; repeat from ★ across to last dc, 2 dc in last dc.

Row 7: Ch 3, turn; dc in first dc, ch 5, sc in next ch-3 sp, (4 dc, ch 1, 4 dc) in next ch-5 sp, sc in next ch-3 sp, ch 5, ★ skip next Cluster, work Cluster, ch 5, sc in next ch-3 sp, (4 dc, ch 1, 4 dc) in next ch-5 sp, sc in next ch-3 sp, ch 5; repeat from ★ across to last 3 sts, skip next 2 sts, 2 dc in last dc.

Row 8: Ch 1, turn; sc in first dc, ch 1, sc in next ch-5 sp, ch 3, skip next sc, work Cluster, 4 dc in next ch-1 sp, work Cluster, ch 3, sc in next ch-5 sp, ★ ch 5, sc in next ch-5 sp, ch 3, skip next sc, work Cluster, 4 dc in next ch-1 sp, work Cluster, ch 3, sc in next ch-5 sp; repeat from ★ across to last 2 dc, ch 1, skip next dc, sc in last dc.

Repeat Rows 5-8 for pattern until piece measures approximately 9{13}"/ 23{33} cm from beginning ch, ending by working Row 8.

Next Row: Ch 3, turn; dc in next ch-1 sp, sc in next ch-3 sp, ch 5, skip next Cluster, work Cluster, ch 5, sc in next ch-3 sp, ★ dc in next ch-5 sp, (ch 1, dc) 7 times in same sp, sc in next ch-3 sp, ch 5, skip next Cluster, work Cluster, ch 5, sc in next ch-3 sp; repeat from ★ across to last ch-1 sp, dc in last ch-1 sp and in last sc.

Edging Rnd (Right side)**:** Turn; slip st in first dc, work Picot, skip next dc, slip st in next sc, ★ † ch 1, (dc, work Picot) 4 times in next ch-5 sp, dc in next ch-5 sp, (work Picot, dc) 3 times in same sp, ch 1, slip st in next sc †, skip next dc, (slip st in next ch-1 sp, work Picot) 6 times, slip st in next ch-1 sp and in next sc; repeat from ★ across to last 2 ch-5 sps, then repeat from † to † once, work Picot, skip next dc, slip in last dc; ch 3, (sc, ch 3) evenly across end of rows; working in free loops of beginning ch ***(Fig. 3, page 30)***, slip st in first ch, [skip next 2 chs, dc in next ch, (ch 1, dc) twice in same ch, skip next 2 chs, slip st in next ch] across; ch 3, (sc, ch 3) evenly across end of rows; join with slip st to first slip st, finish off.

TIE

With Contrasting Color and smaller size hook, chain a 44{47}"/ 112{119.5} cm length; slip st in back ridge of second ch from hook and each ch across ***(Fig. 1, page 30)***; finish off.

Weave Tie through eyelets on Row 2 of Waistband.

Scary Monster

EASY

SHOPPING LIST

Yarn (Medium Weight) MEDIUM 4

[3 ounces, 185 yards
(85 grams, 170 meters) per skein]:

☐ Green (fuzzy yarn) - 1{2} skein(s)

[3.5 ounces, 170 yards
(100 grams, 156 meters) per skein]:

☐ Orange - 1 skein

Crochet Hook

☐ Size I (5.5 mm)
or size needed for gauge

Additional Supplies

☐ Yarn needle

☐ 3/8" (9 mm) wide Ribbon - 1½ yards (1.4 meters)

SIZE INFORMATION

Finished Measurements:

Hat - 16{18¼}"/40.5{46.5} cm circumference

Paws - 6{7}" circumference x 5{6¼}" long [15{18} cm x 12.5{16} cm]

Size Note: We have printed the instructions for the sizes in different colors to make it easier for you to find:

- Size Small (ages 3-5) in Blue
- Size Medium (ages 5-8) in Pink

Instructions in Black apply to both sizes.

GAUGE INFORMATION

12 dc and 7 rows/rnds = 4" (10 cm)

Gauge Swatch: 4" (10 cm) square

With Green, ch 14.

Row 1: Dc in fourth ch from hook **(3 skipped chs count as first dc)** and in each ch across: 12 dc.

Rows 2-7: Ch 3 **(counts as first dc)**, turn; dc in next dc and in each dc across.

Finish off.

STITCH GUIDE

TREBLE CROCHET ***(abbreviated tr)***

YO twice, insert hook in st indicated, YO and pull up a loop (4 loops on hook), (YO and draw through 2 loops on hook) 3 times.

DOUBLE CROCHET 2 TOGETHER ***(abbreviated dc2tog)***

(uses next 2 dc)

★ YO, insert hook in **next** dc, YO and pull up a loop, YO and draw through 2 loops on hook; repeat from ★ once **more**, YO and draw through all 3 loops on hook **(counts as one dc)**.

PAW (Make 2)

With Green and leaving a long end for sewing, ch 20{23}.

Row 1 (Right side)**:** Dc in fourth ch from hook **(3 skipped chs count as first dc)** and in each ch across: 18{21} dc.

Note: Loop a short piece of yarn around any stitch to mark Row 1 as **right** side.

Rows 2 thru 8{10}: Ch 3 **(counts as first dc)**, turn; dc in next dc and in each dc across.

Finish off leaving a long end for sewing.

Trim: With **right** side facing and working in Back Loops Only ***(Fig. 2, page 30)***, join Orange with slip st in first dc; ch 1, hdc in each dc across; finish off leaving a long end for sewing.

Fold Paw in half with **wrong** side together. Using matching colors, whipstitch ends of last 2 rows together ***(Fig. 8b, page 31)***; secure ends.

Using the long end at the bottom of the Paw, whipstitch end of 4{6} rows together, leaving 3 rows open for the thumb; secure end.

HAT

BODY

With Green, ch 4; join with slip st to form a ring.

Rnd 1 (Wrong side)**:** Ch 3 **(counts as first dc, now and throughout)**, 10 dc in ring; join with slip st to first dc: 11 dc.

Note: Loop a short piece of yarn around **back** of any stitch to mark **right** side.

Rnd 2: Ch 3, dc in same st as joining, 2 dc in next dc and in each dc around; join with slip st to first dc: 22 dc.

Rnd 3: Ch 3, dc in same st as joining and in next dc, (2 dc in next dc, dc in next dc) around; join with slip st to first dc: 33 dc.

Rnd 4: Ch 3, dc in same st as joining and in next 2 dc, (2 dc in next dc, dc in next 2 dc) around; join with slip st to first dc: 44 dc.

Rnd 5: Ch 3, dc in same st as joining and in next 3 dc, (2 dc in next dc, dc in next 3 dc) around; join with slip st to first dc: 55 dc.

Rnd 6: Ch 3, dc in same st as joining and in next 10{4} dc, [2 dc in next dc, dc in next 10{4} dc] around; join with slip st to first dc: 60{66} dc.

Rnds 7 thru 10{12}: Ch 3, dc in same st as joining and in each dc around; join with slip st to first dc.

Rnd 11{13}: Ch 3, dc in next 2{3} dc, dc2tog, ★ dc in next 3{4} dc, dc2tog; repeat from ★ around; join with slip st to first dc, finish off: 48{55} dc.

BRIM

Rnd 1: With **right** side facing and working in Back Loops Only *(Fig. 2, page 30)*, join Orange with dc in same st as joining *(see Joining With Dc, page 30)*; dc in next dc and in each dc around; join with slip st to first dc.

Rnd 2: Ch 1, working in both loops, sc in same st as joining and in next 18{22} dc, hdc in next 2 dc, dc in next 2 dc, 3 tr in next dc, dc in next 2 dc, hdc in next 2 dc, sc in each dc around; join with slip st to first sc, finish off.

HAIR

With **right** side facing, join Green with slip st around post of any dc on Rnd 1 of Body; ★ ch 10, slip st around next dc, ch 16, slip st around next dc; repeat from ★ 4 times **more**; join with slip st to first slip st, finish off.

LEFT EAR

Rnd 1: With Green and leaving a long end for sewing, ch 2, 4 sc in second ch from hook; do **not** join, place marker to indicate beginning of rnd *(see Markers, page 29)*.

Work in Back Loops Only throughout Left Ear.

Rnd 2: 2 Sc in each sc around: 8 sc.

Rnd 3: (Hdc in next sc, 2 hdc in next sc) around: 12 hdc.

Rnd 4 (Right side)**:** (Dc in next 2 hdc, 2 dc in next hdc) twice, tr in next hdc, 2 tr in next hdc, leave last 4 hdc unworked; finish off: 11 sts.

Note: Mark Rnd 4 as **right** side.

RIGHT EAR

Rnd 1: With Green and leaving a long end for sewing, ch 2, 4 sc in second ch from hook; do **not** join, place marker to indicate beginning of rnd.

Work in Front Loops Only throughout Right Ear.

Rnd 2: 2 Sc in each sc around: 8 sc.

Rnd 3: (Hdc in next sc, 2 hdc in next sc) around: 12 hdc.

Rnd 4 (Wrong side)**:** (Dc in next 2 hdc, 2 dc in next hdc) twice, tr in next hdc, 2 tr in next hdc, leave last 4 hdc unworked; finish off: 11 sts.

Note: Mark **back** of any stitch on Rnd 4 as **right** side.

Using photo as a guide for placement, sew Ears to Body with straight edge of last rnd facing the front (point of Brim).

TAIL

Rnd 1 (Wrong side)**:** With Green, ch 4, 3 dc in fourth ch from hook **(3 skipped chs count as first dc)**; join with slip st to first dc: 4 dc.

Work on the inside of tube, with the **right** side on the outside.

Rnd 2: Ch 3 **(counts as first dc, now and throughout)**, dc in same st as joining and in next dc, 2 dc in next dc, dc in last dc; join with slip st to first dc: 6 dc.

Rnd 3: Ch 3, dc in same st as joining and in next 2 dc, 2 dc in next dc, dc in last 2 dc; join with slip st to first dc: 8 dc.

Rnd 4: Ch 3, 2 dc in next dc, dc in next dc, hdc in next dc, sc in next dc, hdc in next dc, dc in next dc, 2 dc in last dc; join with slip st to first dc: 10 sts.

Rnd 5: Ch 3, 2 dc in next dc, dc in next 2 dc, hdc in next hdc, sc in next sc, hdc in next hdc, dc in next 2 dc, 2 dc in last dc; join with slip st to first dc: 12 sts.

Rnd 6: Ch 3, (2 dc in next dc, dc in next dc) twice, hdc in next hdc, sc in next sc, hdc in next hdc, (dc in next dc, 2 dc in next dc) twice; join with slip st to first dc: 16 sts.

Rnd 7: Ch 3, (2 dc in next dc, dc in next dc) 3 times, hdc in next hdc, sc in next sc, hdc in next hdc, (dc in next dc, 2 dc in next dc) 3 times; join with slip st to first dc: 22 sts.

Rnds 8 and 9: Ch 3, dc in next dc and in each st around; join with slip st to first dc.

Rnd 10: Ch 3, dc in next 5 dc, 2 dc in next dc, dc in next 2 dc, 2 dc in next dc, dc in next 3 dc, 2 dc in next dc, dc in next 2 dc, 2 dc in next dc, dc in last 5 dc; join with slip st to first dc: 26 dc.

Rnds 11 and 12: Ch 3, dc in next dc and in each dc around; join with slip st to first dc.

Finish off.

Last Row (Right side)**:** Flatten last rnd with joining at center back and tip of tail curved toward you. Working through **both** layers, join Orange with dc in first dc ***(see Joining With Dc, page 30)***; dc in next dc and in each dc across; finish off: 13 dc.

SCALES

With Orange and leaving a long end for sewing, ch 26.

Row 1: Slip st in second ch from hook, ★ sc in next ch, hdc in next ch, dc in next ch, tr in next ch, dc in next ch, hdc in next ch, sc in next ch, slip st in next ch; repeat from ★ 2 times **more**; finish off.

Using photo as a guide for placement, sew beginning ch of Scales across rows of Tail.

TUMMY

With Orange, ch 10.

Rnd 1 (Right side)**:** 2 Dc in fourth ch from hook (**3 skipped chs count as first dc**), dc in next 5 chs, 5 dc in last ch; working in free loops of beginning ch ***(Fig. 3, page 30)***, dc in next 5 chs, 2 dc in next ch; join with slip st to first dc: 20 dc.

Note: Loop a short piece of yarn around any stitch to mark Rnd 1 as **right** side.

Rnd 2: Ch 3 (**counts as first dc, now and throughout**), dc in same st as joining, 2 dc in each of next 3 dc, dc in next 3 dc, 2 dc in each of next 7 dc, dc in next 3 dc, 2 dc in each of last 3 dc; join with slip st to first dc: 34 dc.

Rnd 3: Ch 3, 2 dc in next dc, (dc in next dc, 2 dc in next dc) 3 times, dc in next 4 dc, 2 dc in next dc, (dc in next dc, 2 dc in next dc) 6 times, dc in next 4 dc, 2 dc in next dc, (dc in next dc, 2 dc in next dc) twice; join with slip st to first dc: 48 dc.

Rnd 4: Ch 3, dc in same st as joining and in next 3 dc, (2 dc in next dc, dc in next 3 dc) around; join with slip st to first dc, finish off: 60 dc.

Rnd 5: With **right** side facing and working in Back Loops Only ***(Fig. 2, page 30)***, join Green with sc in same st as joining ***(see Joining With Sc, page 30)***; sc in same st and in next 4 dc, (2 sc in next dc, sc in next 4 dc) around; join with slip st to first sc: 72 sc.

Rnd 6: ★ Ch 10, skip next 2 sc, slip st in both loops of next sc; repeat from ★ around working last slip st in joining slip st; finish off.

To join Tail and Tummy, weave ribbon through spaces on last row of Tail, then through dc across top of Rnd 4 of Tummy; tie ribbon in a bow at side.

Super Hero

EASY

SHOPPING LIST

Yarn (Medium Weight) MEDIUM 4
[6 ounces, 315 yards
(170 grams, 288 meters) per skein]:

- ☐ Red - 1 skein
- ☐ Blue - 1 skein
- ☐ Black - 1 skein

Crochet Hooks

- ☐ Size F (3.75 mm)
- ☐ Size H (5 mm)
  or sizes needed for gauge

Additional Supplies

- ☐ Sewing needle and thread
- ☐ Buttons - 2

SIZE INFORMATION

Finished Measurements:

Cape - 12{13½}" wide x 14{18}" long [30.5{34.5} cm x 35.5{45.5} cm]
Boots - 6{7}"/15{18} cm circumference
Armband - 2¼" (5.5 cm) wide

Size Note: We have printed the instructions for the sizes in different colors to make it easier for you to find:

- Size Small (ages 3-5) in Blue
- Size Medium (ages 5-8) in Pink

Instructions in Black apply to both sizes.

GAUGE INFORMATION

With larger size hook,
15 dc = 4" (10 cm),
8 rows = 3¾" (9.5 cm)
With smaller size hook,
8 dc = 2" (5 cm),
4 rows = 1¾" (4.5 cm)

Gauge Swatch: 4" wide x 3¾" high (10 cm x 9.5 cm)

With larger size hook, ch 17.

Row 1: Dc in fourth ch from hook **(3 skipped chs count as first dc)** and in each ch across: 15 dc.

Rows 2-8: Ch 3 **(counts as first dc)**, turn; dc in next dc and in each dc across.

Finish off.

STITCH GUIDE

DOUBLE CROCHET 2 TOGETHER ***(abbreviated dc2tog)*** (uses next 2 dc)
★ YO, insert hook in **next** dc, YO and pull up a loop, YO and draw through 2 loops on hook; repeat from ★ once **more**, YO and draw through all 3 loops on hook **(counts as one dc)**.

DOUBLE CROCHET 3 TOGETHER ***(abbreviated dc3tog)*** (uses next 3 sts)
★ YO, insert hook in **next** st, YO and pull up a loop, YO and draw through 2 loops on hook; repeat from ★ 2 times **more**, YO and draw through all 4 loops on hook.

5-DC CLUSTER (uses next 5 sts)
★ YO, insert hook in **next** st, YO and pull up a loop, YO and draw through 2 loops on hook; repeat from ★ 4 times **more**, YO and draw through all 6 loops on hook.

LONG CLUSTER (uses 5 sts)
† YO, insert hook in **next** dc, YO and pull up a loop, YO and draw through 2 loops on hook †; repeat from † to † once **more**, YO, working **around** previous 2 rows, insert hook in **both** loops of center dc of 5-dc group on Row 1 ***(Fig. A)***, YO and pull up a loop even with loops on hook, YO and draw through 2 loops on hook, repeat from † to † twice, YO and draw through all 6 loops on hook.

Fig. A

REVERSE SINGLE CROCHET ***(abbreviated reverse sc)***
Working from **left** to **right**, insert hook in st to right of hook ***(Fig. B)***, YO and draw through, under and to left of loop on hook (2 loops on hook) ***(Fig. C)***, YO and draw through both loops on hook ***(Figs. D & E)***.

Fig. B

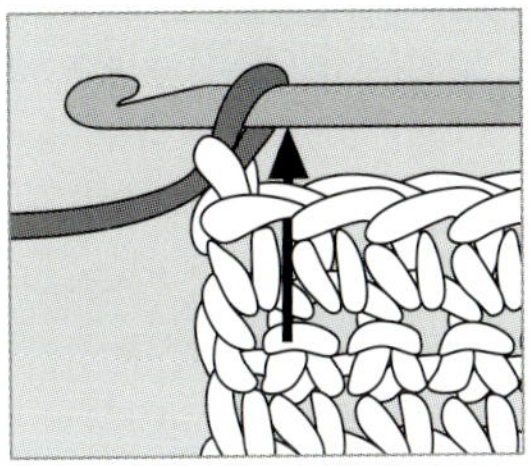

Fig. C

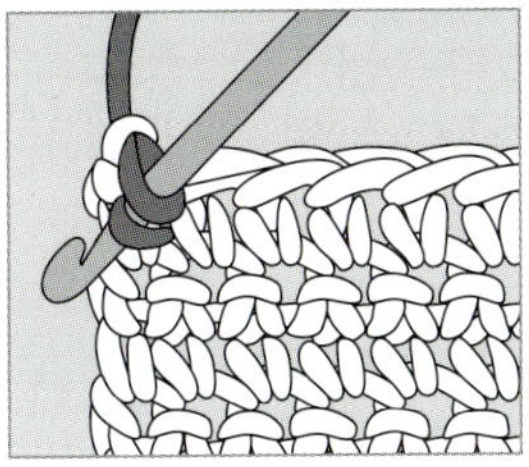

Fig. D

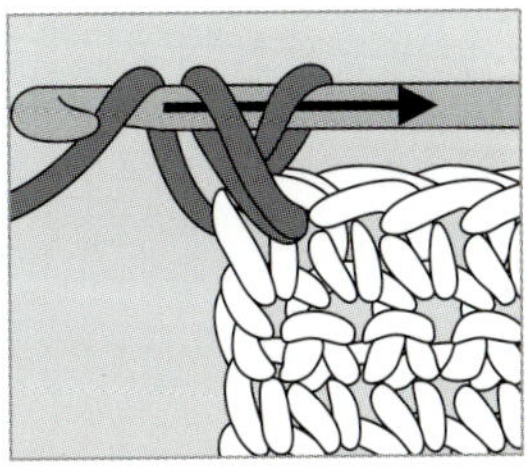

Fig. E

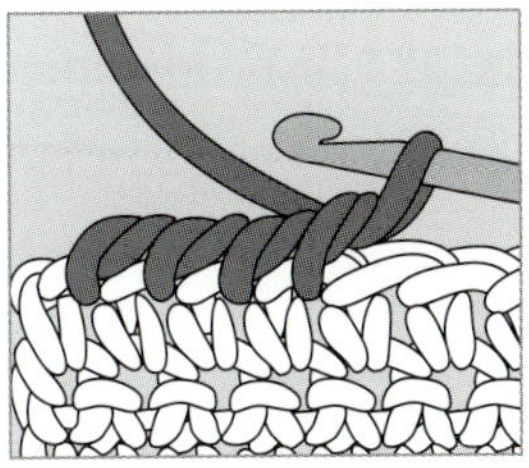

CAPE

BAND

With smaller size hook and Red, ch 56{67}.

Row 1 (Right side)**:** Dc in fourth ch from hook **(3 skipped chs count as first dc)** and in next 2{3} chs, **[**2 dc in next ch, dc in next 4{5} chs**]** 10 times: 64{75} dc.

Note: Loop a short piece of yarn around any stitch to mark Row 1 as **right** side.

Row 2: Ch 3 **(counts as first dc, now and throughout)**, turn; dc in next dc, ch 2, skip next 2 dc **(buttonhole made)**, dc in next 4{5} dc, 2 dc in next dc, **[**dc in next 5{6} dc, 2 dc in next dc**]** 8 times, dc in last 7{9} dc: 71{82} dc and one ch-2 sp.

Row 3: Ch 3, turn; dc in next 10{13} dc, 2 dc in next dc, **[**dc in next 6{7} dc, 2 dc in next dc**]** 7 times, dc in next 8{9} dc, 2 dc in next ch-2 sp, dc in last 2 dc: 81{92} dc.

Row 4: Ch 1, turn; sc in first 8 dc, hdc in next 8 dc, dc in next 9{12} dc, 2 dc in next dc, **[**dc in next 4 dc, 2 dc in next dc**]** 6{7} times, dc in next 9{12} dc, hdc in next 8 dc, sc in next 8 dc; finish off: 88{100} sts.

BODY

Row 1: With **right** side facing and using larger size hook, skip first 20{23} sts and join Red with slip st in next dc; sc in next dc, hdc in next dc, dc in next 21{24} dc, 2 dc in next dc, dc in next 20{23} dc, hdc in next dc, sc in next dc, slip st in next dc, leave remaining 20{23} sts unworked: 49{55} sts.

Row 2: Turn; skip first slip st, slip st in next 3 sts, ch 3, dc in next dc and in each dc across to last 3 sts, leave last 3 sts unworked: 43{49} dc.

Row 3: Ch 3, turn; dc in next dc and in each dc across.

Repeat Row 3 until piece measures approximately 11{15}"/28{38} cm from beginning ch **or** 3" (7.5 cm) less than desired length, ending by working a **right** side row; do **not** finish off.

BOTTOM BORDER

Row 1: Ch 3, turn; 2 dc in first dc, skip next 2 dc, sc in next dc, ★ skip next 2 dc, 5 dc in next dc, skip next 2 dc, sc in next dc; repeat from ★ across to last 3 dc, skip next 2 dc, 3 dc in last dc changing to Blue in last dc made ***(Fig. 7a, page 31)***; do **not** cut Red: 7{8} sc and 8{9} dc groups.

Row 2: Ch 1, turn; working in Front Loops Only ***(Fig. 2, page 30)***, sc in first dc, ★ ch 2, work 5-dc Cluster, ch 2, sc in next dc; repeat from ★ across: 8{9} sc and 7{8} Clusters.

Row 3: Turn; working in both loops, slip st in first sc, skip next ch, 5 dc in next ch, ★ skip next Cluster and next ch-2 sp, slip st in next sc, skip next ch, 5 dc in next ch; repeat from ★ across to last Cluster; cut Blue, skip last Cluster and ch-2 sp, with Red, slip st in last sc: 7{8} 5-dc groups.

Row 4: Ch 2 **(does not count as a st)**, turn; working in Back Loops Only, dc2tog, (dc, sc, dc) in next dc, ★ work Long Cluster, (dc, sc, dc) in next dc; repeat from ★ across to last 2 dc, dc3tog: 29{33} sts.

Row 5: Ch 3, turn; working in both loops, dc in first st, (dc in next dc, 2 dc in next st) across to last 2 dc, dc in last 2 dc; finish off: 43{49} dc.

TRIM

With **right** side facing and working from **left** to **right** in end of rows on Body, join Blue with slip st in Row 1; ch 1, work reverse sc evenly around entire cape ***(Figs. B-E, page 25)***, working in free loops of beginning ch ***(Fig. 3, page 30)***; join with slip st to first st, finish off.

Sew button to Band opposite buttonhole.

BOOT (Make 2)

FOOT & LEG

With larger size hook and Black, ch 11{13}.

Rnd 1 (Right side)**:** 3 Sc in second ch from hook, sc in next 8{10} chs, 3 sc in last ch; working in free loops of beginning ch *(Fig. 3, page 30)*, sc in next 8{10} chs; do **not** join: 22{26} sc.

Hdc in next sc, working in continuous rnds, dc in each st around until Boot measures 9{11½}"/23{29} cm from beginning ch **or** to desired length, ending at fold when Boot is flattened with center sc of both 3-sc groups on Rnd 1 at sides.

Place marker before next dc to indicate beginning of rnds *(see Markers, page 29)*.

TOP SHAPING & TRIM

Rnd 1: Dc in next 2{3} dc, hdc in next dc, sc in next dc, slip st in next 3 dc, sc in next dc, hdc in next dc, dc in next 13{16} dc.

Rnd 2: Dc in next 2{3} dc, hdc in next 2 sts, sc in next slip st, slip st in next slip st, sc in next slip st, hdc in next 2 sts, dc in next 13{16} dc.

Rnd 3: Dc in next 2{3} dc, hdc in next hdc, sc in next hdc, slip st in next sc, skip next slip st, slip st in next sc, sc in next hdc, hdc in next hdc, dc in next 7{9} dc, 3 dc in next dc, dc in next 2{3} dc, hdc in next dc, sc in next dc, slip st in next dc; finish off: 23{27} sts.

Rnd 4: With **right** side facing, join Red with sc in last slip st *(see Joining With Sc, page 30)*; sc in next 5{6} sts, slip st in next slip st, sc in next 10{12} sts, 3 sc in next dc, sc in last 5{6} sts; cut Red, with Blue, join with slip st to first sc *(Fig. 7b, page 31)*: 25{29} sts.

Rnd 5: Ch 1, sc in same st as joining and in next 5{6} sc, slip st in next slip st, sc in next 11{13} sc, 3 sc in next sc, sc in last 6{7} sc; join with slip st to first sc, finish off: 27{31} sts.

ARMBAND

Row 1: With smaller size hook and Blue, ch 4, dc in fourth ch from hook **(3 skipped chs count as first dc)**: 2 dc.

Row 2: Ch 3 **(counts as first dc, now and throughout)**, turn; dc in first dc, 2 dc in last dc: 4 dc.

Row 3: Ch 3, turn; dc in first 3 dc, 2 dc in last dc: 6 dc.

Row 4: Ch 3, turn; dc in first 2 dc, ch 2, skip next 2 dc **(buttonhole made)**, dc in next dc, 2 dc in last dc: 6 dc and one ch-2 sp.

Row 5: Ch 3, turn; dc in next 2 dc, 2 dc in next ch-2 sp, dc in last 3 dc: 8 dc.

Row 6: Ch 3, turn; dc in next dc and in each dc across.

Repeat Row 6, 12{14} times **or** to desired length.

Finish off.

Trim (Right side)**:** Using smaller size hook, join Red with slip st in fifth dc on last row; working from **left** to **right**, work reverse sc evenly around entire armband ***(Figs. B-E, page 25)***, working in free loops of beginning ch ***(Fig. 3, page 30)***; join with slip st to first st, finish off.

Sew button to center of last dc row.

General Instructions

ABBREVIATIONS

BLO	Back Loop(s) Only
BPdc	Back Post double crochet(s)
ch(s)	chain(s)
cm	centimeters
dc	double crochet(s)
dc2tog	double crochet 2 together
dc3tog	double crochet 3 together
FLO	Front Loop(s) Only
FPdc	Front Post double crochet(s)
hdc	half double crochet(s)
mm	millimeters
Rnd(s)	Round(s)
sc	single crochet(s)
sp(s)	space(s)
st(s)	stitch(es)
tr	treble crochet
YO	yarn over

SYMBOLS & TERMS

★ — work instructions following ★ as many **more** times as indicated in addition to the first time.

† to † — work all instructions from first † to second † **as many** times as specified.

( ) or **[ ]** — work enclosed instructions **as many** times as specified by the number immediately following **or** work all enclosed instructions in the stitch or space indicated **or** contains explanatory remarks.

colon (:) — the number(s) given after a colon at the end of a row or round denote(s) the number of stitches or spaces you should have on that row or round.

GAUGE

Exact gauge is essential for proper fit. Before beginning your project, make the sample swatch given in the individual instructions in the yarn and hook specified. After completing the swatch, measure it, counting your stitches and rows carefully. If your swatch is larger or smaller than specified, **make another, changing hook size to get the correct gauge**. Keep trying until you find the size hook that will give you the specified gauge.

MARKERS

Markers are used to help distinguish the beginning of each round being worked. Place a 2" (5 cm) scrap piece of yarn before the first stitch of each round, moving marker after each round is complete.

Yarn Weight Symbol & Names	LACE 0	SUPER FINE 1	FINE 2	LIGHT 3	MEDIUM 4	BULKY 5	SUPER BULKY 6	JUMBO 7
Type of Yarns in Category	Fingering, size 10 crochet thread	Sock, Fingering, Baby	Sport, Baby	DK, Light Worsted	Worsted, Afghan, Aran	Chunky, Craft, Rug	Super Bulky, Roving	Jumbo, Roving
Crochet Gauge* Ranges in Single Crochet to 4" (10 cm)	32-42 sts**	21-32 sts	16-20 sts	12-17 sts	11-14 sts	8-11 sts	6-9 sts	5 sts and fewer
Advised Hook Size Range	Steel*** 6 to 8, Regular hook B-1	B-1 to E-4	E-4 to 7	7 to I-9	I-9 to K-10½	K-10½ to M/N-13	M/N-13 to Q	Q and larger

*GUIDELINES ONLY: The chart above reflects the most commonly used gauges and hook sizes for specific yarn categories.

** Lace weight yarns are usually crocheted with larger hooks to create lacy openwork patterns. Accordingly, a gauge range is difficult to determine. Always follow the gauge stated in your pattern.

*** Steel crochet hooks are sized differently from regular hooks–the higher the number, the smaller the hook, which is the reverse of regular hook sizing.

CROCHET TERMINOLOGY

UNITED STATES		INTERNATIONAL
slip stitch (slip st)	=	single crochet (sc)
single crochet (sc)	=	double crochet (dc)
half double crochet (hdc)	=	half treble crochet (htr)
double crochet (dc)	=	treble crochet (tr)
treble crochet (tr)	=	double treble crochet (dtr)
double treble crochet (dtr)	=	triple treble crochet (ttr)
triple treble crochet (tr tr)	=	quadruple treble crochet (qtr)
skip	=	miss

CROCHET HOOKS

U.S.	B-1	C-2	D-3	E-4	F-5	G-6	7	H-8	I-9	J-10	K-10½	L-11	M/N-13	N/P-15	P/Q	Q	S
Metric - mm	2.25	2.75	3.25	3.5	3.75	4	4.5	5	5.5	6	6.5	8	9	10	15	16	19

JOINING WITH SC

When instructed to join with sc, begin with a slip knot on hook. Insert hook in stitch or space indicated, YO and pull up a loop, YO and draw through both loops on hook.

JOINING WITH DC

When instructed to join with dc, begin with a slip knot on hook. YO, holding loop on hook, insert hook in stitch or space indicated, YO and pull up a loop (3 loops on hook), (YO and draw through 2 loops on hook) twice.

BACK RIDGE

Work only in loops indicated by arrows *(Fig. 1)*.

Fig. 1

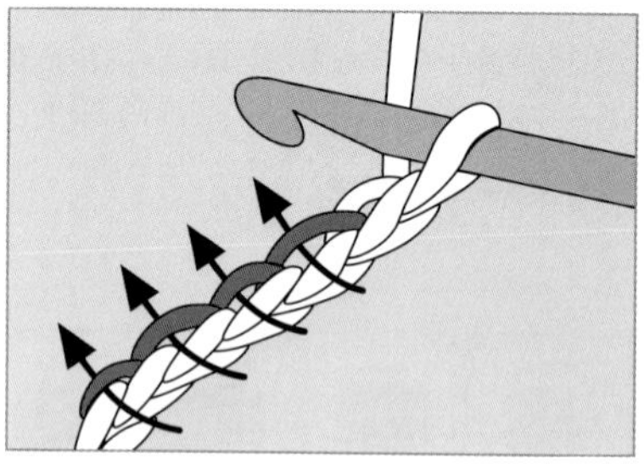

BACK OR FRONT LOOP ONLY

Work only in loop(s) indicated by arrow *(Fig. 2)*.

Fig. 2

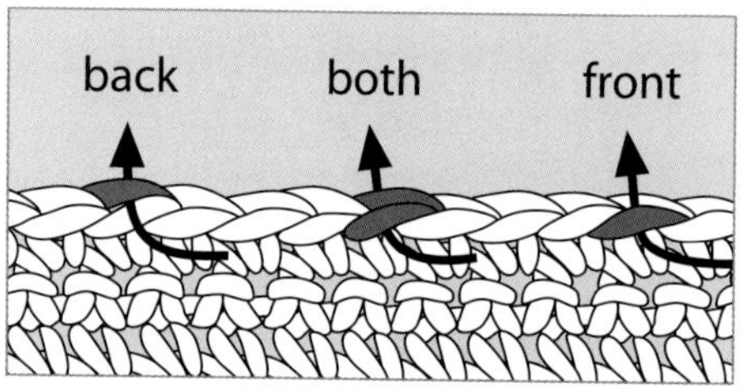

FREE LOOPS OF A CHAIN

When instructed to work in free loops of a chain, work in loop indicated by arrow *(Fig. 3)*.

Fig. 3

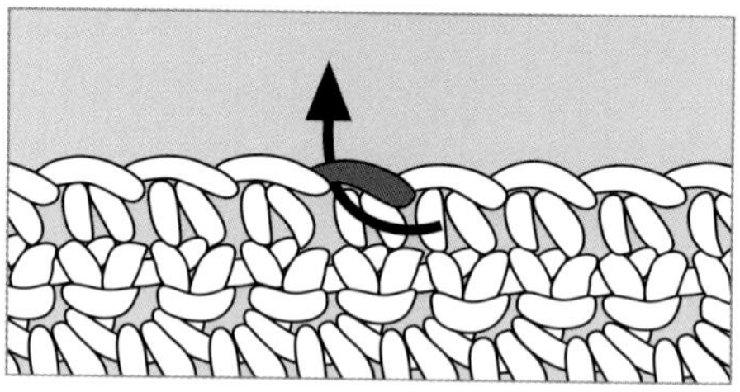

FRONT POST DOUBLE CROCHET *(abbreviated FPdc)*

YO, insert hook from **front** to **back** around post of st indicated *(Fig. 4a)*, YO and pull up a loop *(Fig. 4b)* (3 loops on hook), (YO and draw through 2 loops on hook) twice.

Fig. 4a

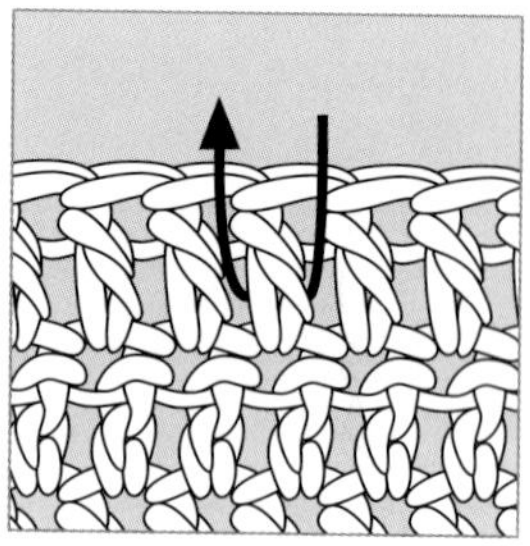

Fig. 4b

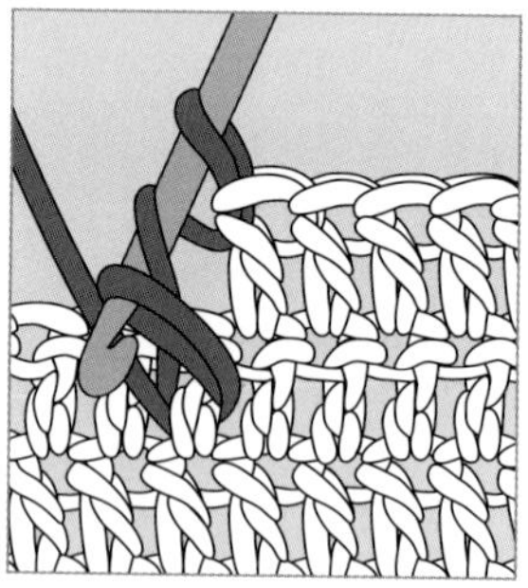

BEGINNER	Projects for first-time crocheters using basic stitches. Minimal shaping.
EASY	Projects using yarn with basic stitches, repetitive stitch patterns, simple color changes, and simple shaping and finishing.
INTERMEDIATE	Projects using a variety of techniques, such as basic lace patterns or color patterns, mid-level shaping and finishing.
EXPERIENCED	Projects with intricate stitch patterns, techniques and dimension, such as non-repeating patterns, multi-color techniques, fine threads, small hooks, detailed shaping and refined finishing.

BACK POST DOUBLE CROCHET *(abbreviated BPdc)*

YO, insert hook from **back** to **front** around post of st indicated *(Fig. 5a)*, YO and pull up a loop *(Fig. 5b)* (3 loops on hook), (YO and draw through 2 loops on hook) twice.

Fig. 5a

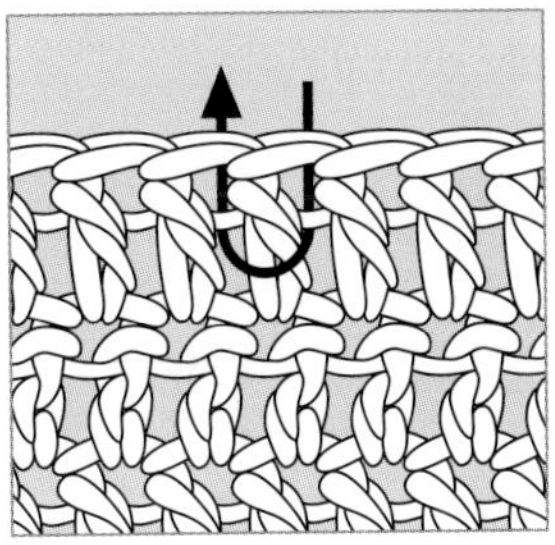

Fig. 5b

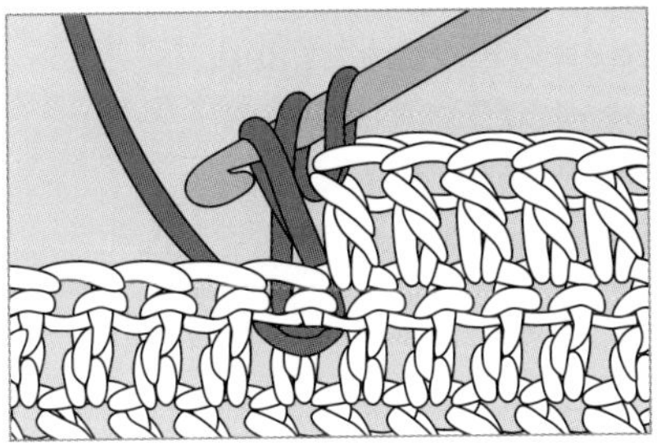

WORKING IN FRONT OF OR AROUND A STITCH

Work in stitch or space indicated, inserting hook in direction of arrow *(Fig. 6)*.

Fig. 6

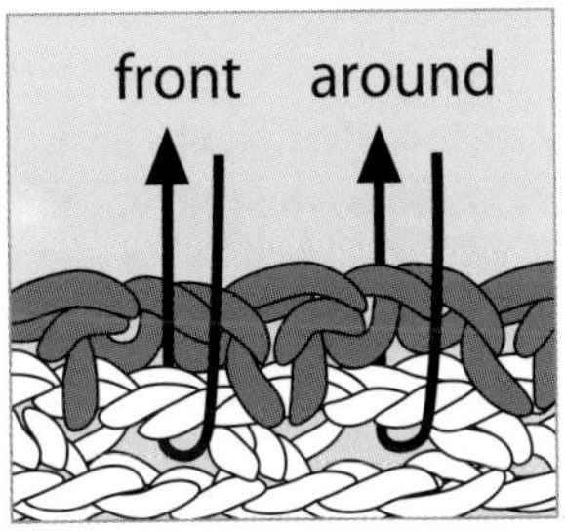

CHANGING COLORS

To change colors while working a dc, YO, insert hook in stitch indicated, YO and pull up a loop, YO and draw through 2 loops on hook, drop yarn, with new yarn *(Fig. 7a)*, YO and draw through 2 loops on hook.

Fig. 7a

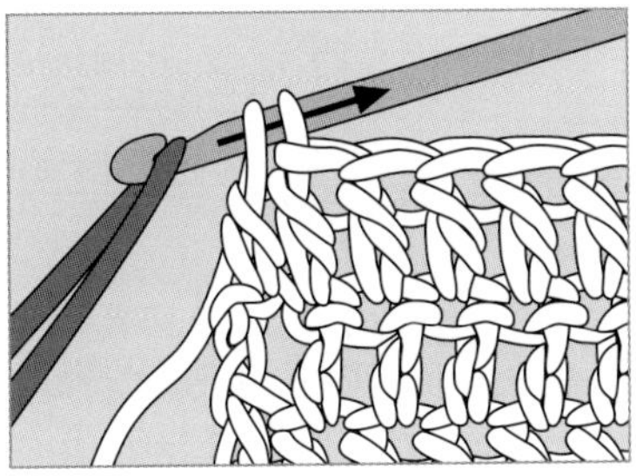

To change colors while joining with a slip st, drop yarn, insert hook in first stitch, hook new yarn and draw through st and loop on hook *(Fig. 7b)*.

Fig. 7b

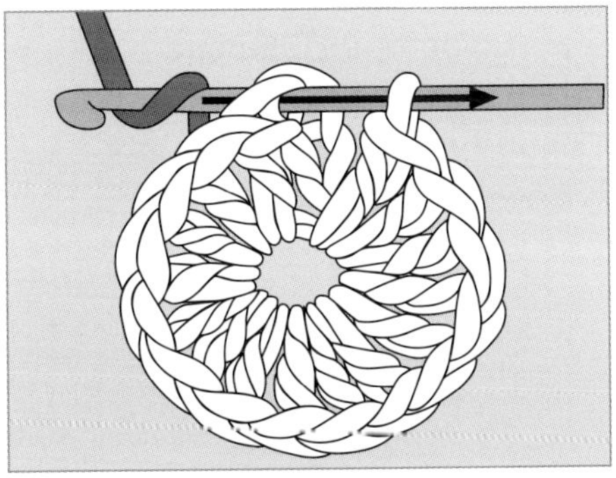

WHIPSTITCH

With **wrong** sides together, sew through both pieces once to secure the beginning of the seam, leaving an ample yarn end to weave in later. Insert the needle from **right** to **left** through two strands on each stitch of each piece *(Fig. 8a)* **or** through ends of rows *(Fig. 8b)*. Bring the needle around and insert it from **right** to **left** through the next strands on both pieces.

Repeat along the edge, being careful to match stitches and rows.

Fig. 8a

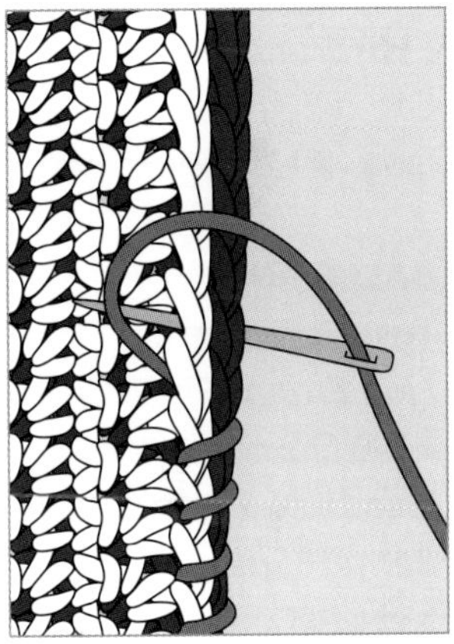

Fig. 8b

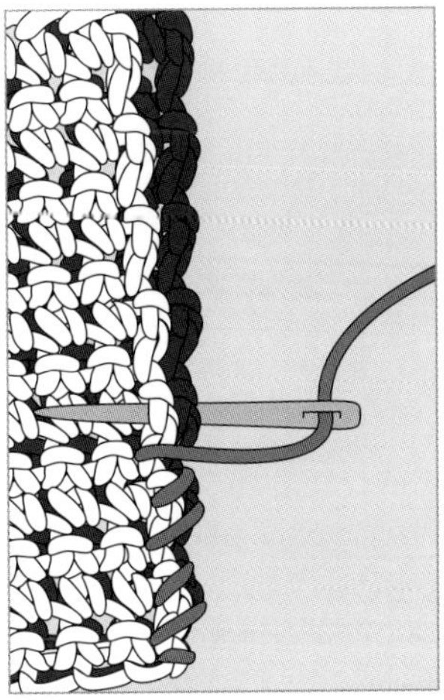

Yarn Information

The items in this book were made using a variety of yarns. Any brand of the specific weight of yarn may be used. It is best to refer to the yardage/meters when determining how many balls or skeins to purchase. Remember, to arrive at the finished size, it is the GAUGE/TENSION that is important, not the brand of yarn.

For your convenience, listed below are the yarns used to create our photography models. Because yarn manufacturers make frequent changes in their product lines, you may sometimes find it necessary to use a substitute yarn or to search for the discontinued product at alternate suppliers (locally or online).

ANIMALS
Lion Brand® Vanna's Choice®
Cat - #149 Silver Grey
Dog - #130 Honey
Monkey - #124 Toffee
Lion Brand® Fun Fur®
Cat - #204 Lava
Dog - #125 Tigers Eye

BALLERINA
Tutu & Flowers
Lion Brand® Shawl in a Ball®
#300 Om Opal
Headband & Leg Warmers
Bernat® Satin Sparkle™
#53424 Coral

PRINCESS
Crown
Patons® Metallic™
Main Color - #97005 Moonstone
Contrasting Color - #95134 Blue Steel
Cape
Red Heart® Gumdrop®
Main Color - #0530 Blueberry
Caron® Simply Soft®
Contrasting Color - #9709 Light Country Blue
Sweetheart Overskirt
Lion Brand® Vanna's Glamour®
Main Color - #100 Diamond
Caron® Simply Soft®
Contrasting Color - #9709 Light Country Blue

SCARY MONSTER
Lion Brand® Vanna's Complement
Green - #172 Kelly Green
Lion Brand® Vanna's Choice®
Orange - #134 Terra Cotta

SUPER HERO
Caron® Simply Soft®
Red - #9763 Harvest Red
Blue - #9759 Ocean
Black - #9727 Black

We have made every effort to ensure that these instructions are accurate and complete. We cannot, however, be responsible for human error, typographical mistakes, or variations in individual work.

Items made and instructions tested by Janet Akins.

Production Team: Instructional/Technical Editor - Cathy Hardy; Editorial Writer - Susan Frantz Wiles; Senior Graphic Artist - Lora Puls; Photo Stylist - Stephanie Moore; and Photographer - Jason Masters.